Weak Devotions

For Melanie —

Weak Devotions

poems

Luke Hankins

Luke Hankins

With gratitude for your support.

WIPF & STOCK · Eugene, Oregon

See you on the dance floor!

— Luke

1-12-11

WEAK DEVOTIONS
poems

Copyright © 2011 Luke Hankins. All rights reserved. Except for brief quotations in critical publications or reviews, no part of this book may be reproduced in any manner without prior written permission from the publisher. Write: Permissions, Wipf and Stock Publishers, 199 W. 8th Ave., Suite 3, Eugene, OR 97401.

Wipf & Stock
An Imprint of Wipf and Stock Publishers
199 W. 8th Ave., Suite 3
Eugene, OR 97401

www.wipfandstock.com

ISBN 13: 978-1-61097-725-8

Manufactured in the U.S.A.

Cover art by Makoto Fujimura (in situ photograph; azurite, malachite, and vermillion on kumohada taken by the artist in the studio while wet). Reproduced by permission of the artist. www.makotofujimura.com

Contents

Contents

Acknowledgments

I am grateful to the editors of the following publications, in which the listed poems originally appeared, sometimes in earlier versions:

American Literary Review: "A Shape With Forty Wings"
Asheville Poetry Review: "Earthly Kingdom"
Connotation Press: An Online Artifact: "Choirmaster," "Conductor's Prayer," "Amateur's Prayer," "The Old Preacher Prays," and "Herald"
The Cortland Review: "Please Follow the Instructions"
The Hampden–Sydney Poetry Review: "I Shocked the Hills" and "Lament"
Marginalia: "The Fact"
The Other Journal: "Blood" and "Hedonist's Prayer"
Poetry East: "Sojourner's Prayer" and "Weak Devotions"
Ruminate: "Newspaper Photo"
Southern Poetry Review: "Floccinaucinihilipilification"
Sow's Ear Poetry Review: "Patient's Prayer"
Verse Libre Quarterly (now defunct): "Wisteria"

"Weak Devotions" also appeared as a reprint on the blog of the National Public Radio radio program *Being* (http://onbeing.org).

"Blood" also appeared as a reprint in the anthology *Remembering the Future: Essays, Interviews, and Poetry at the Intersections of Theology and Culture* (Cascade Books, 2009).

"Choirmaster" and "Failure" were broadcast on the radio program *The Poet's Weave* on WFIU Public Radio in Bloomington, Indiana, and the program is archived online at http://indianapublicmedia.org/poetsweave/.

Acknowledgments

Personal Thanks

For their invaluable assistance in revising these poems and this collection, and for their great dedication of time and energy, my enduring gratitude to Keith Flynn, Stephen Haven, Elizabeth Hoover, Maurice Manning, Ashley Anna McHugh, and Chad Prevost. For their guidance and encouragement, I acknowledge my teachers: JoLynn Goffin, Chad Prevost, and Maurice Manning. My love to my parents and siblings, who have always offered support and enthusiasm: my father, Carl Hankins; my mother, Laura Hankins–Rand; my sisters, Janna Wardle and Carly Borders; and my brother, Joey Hankins.

Soli Deo gloria.

Weak Devotions

. . . We be cast low; for why? the sportfull love
of our great Maker (like as mothers dear
in pleasance from them do their children shove
that back again they may recoyl more near)
shoves of our soules a while, the more them to endear.

—Henry More, "The Preexistency of the Soul"

For, if I imp my wing on thine,
Affliction shall advance the flight in me.

—George Herbert, "Easter Wings"

We are created by being destroyed.

—Franz Wright, "Letter"

I.

A Shape with Forty Wings

EARTHLY KINGDOM

I.

Creekmuck crawfish,
                    shitstenched mudbugs
                                        swarming in the murk—
we set raw meat on nets
                    to see how many we could catch,
to cup
        the smallest crayspawn in our palms,
                                        wriggling open then shut.

Of Louisiana's armored animals—
                                armadillo, rolypoly,
                                        alligator snapping turtle—
of all shellcased hiders, carapace-duckers,
                                crawfish were the ones with claws,
and we'd allow the smaller ones
                        to pinch us and dangle from our skin.

        And there were, of course, those armored falcons
                                        diving at us in our dreams,
                native ravagers sent in our sleep
                                to wake us to the fear of death.

II.

Bright cardinal,
                red-feathered raptor
                                on the berried branch,
        little dinosaur,
                        you cock your crested head
to see—
        you plunge your thorn-like beak.

            ~

3

Coiled spring, you freeze
                         then chirp and leap,
          hopping on your wings through air.

God's little toy,
               mesozoic wind-up—
         what a pragmatic bit
                   of precise mechanical joy.

III.

Whitemouthed death living among us,
                             black length of muscle,
fanged wrangler with the mud,
                    slick pondswimmer, streamwanderer,
watermoccassin—
              I watched my father slice a shovel through you
just below the skull—
              death, thou shalt die, I had read—
                           and yet
when I remembered you in dreams, the way you wrung yourself
like a piece of rope that thought it was a hand, when I watched
that grasping over and again I knew that if even death itself
was doomed to die certainly I could not hope to escape.

IV.

On Good Friday the dogs were after crawfish in the creek—
they muddied up their shaggy hair,
                       they dragged their jaws through silt
and shallow water,
             they ate the mud itself along with their prey.
We hosed them down and hoped they wouldn't vomit in the house
when they had dried.
               I watched cardinals hunting food and singing
in the yard, the dogs huffing on the sun-hot patio.
                        I brought the dogs inside,
but one was limping now
             and looking down with glazed eyes.
We noticed a swollen leg, and laid the trembling dog down

as he died.
>*Cottonmouth*, dad said.

~

I knew the prayers we'd been brought up to say—
Your kingdom come,
>*your will be done on earth*
>>*as it is in heaven.*

I took dad's shovel and dug a hole big enough for a kid like me.
There were roots and stones, so it took hours.
>Dad had come out
to say he would finish it, then later that it was big enough,
but I wouldn't let him stop me. I kept on digging,
>thinking *Whose will is this?*

I finally went inside. My hands had blistered
and the blisters had broken against the handle
and they were raw and bleeding. I rinsed my hands
and bandaged them.
>I remember thinking about Christ, trying to make
myself mean it as I said
>*Well, damn—if God can die, then so can I*
>>before I fell asleep.

LOUISIANA

In Pineville, Dad would chop the heads
of cottonmouths off with a flat-head shovel
and the bodies would spurt blood and writhe
as if in anger. I almost had my head taken off
by a flat-head shovel in the hands of a neighbor boy—
no lie—and was pissed on by another—
and who knows why? Once, I watched a 5-year-old
pull the trigger of a pellet gun
aimed at the belly of another boy
and he ran screaming up the hill to his house.
We learned later that the lead curved upwards
and almost reached his heart, almost killed him.
The police officer questioned me the next day
in my home, and I identified the weapon—
identical to one I used to hunt snakes in the creek.
After telling him of the eerie proclamation
I witnessed—"I'm going to shoot you"—
and the immediate, reasonless violence that followed,
I cried, then lay on Mother's lap in silence on the couch.
I imagined the holes tunneled through his liver
by the hot metal hungry for his heart
and I renounced my own rifle.

INVENTORY

Rusted cans, split bottles,
fallen branches and spilt nails,
busted fence-posts, stones
and scraps of steel,
heavy tire rims, broken rails, strings
of barbed wire and a thousand
things that catch fire
or that swing or sting
or separate bones with their weight . . .
If you know how to look,
there are weapons everywhere.

BLOOD

I've drawn blood
from others, in my childhood,
even friends and kin—
slit the heavy garment
of skin or split sinus caves
with my hard fist.

Very young, I cried
if my sister hurt herself.
Later, her hot blood slicked
my hammering hand—
that hurt was, more
than hers, my own.
And she wept for me.

THE FACT

*I bought an Animal Facts book at the zoo. One
of my favorite facts is the one about the shrew.*
—from my 3rd-grade journal

I wonder what made me think my teacher knew
which fact about the shrew I was referring to.
Since she knew me, perhaps I thought she would have guessed
that I meant the one about the heart, which, at rest,
beats as fast as eight hundred times each minute,
which seemed to me a number almost infinite,
though I would have bet my nervous heart
could have rivaled it when thoughts of death would not depart.
But, perhaps it was the way
the shrew will find a place to stay—
the burrow of a rat or mouse,
unafraid to show up uninvited at a neighbor's house.
Then again, I must have been thinking of its metabolic rate
which condemns it to a hungry fate
(like the one I knew so well), so that if it doesn't eat
for half a day, its lightning heart will cease to beat.
Though I could have had in mind its lightness,
the way the water shrew can walk as if weightless
for a short space on the surface of a pond.
In the end, however, I wonder if I was simply fond
of the familiar fragility of this animal, who, I read,
at a sudden noise might just drop dead.

WHEN I WAS A CHILD, I REASONED AS A CHILD

In Louisiana, when we were boys,
      we studied to be men.
We broke through woods and hunted snakes,
      we made an awful din.

When we were boys we fought until
      we thought that we had won.
We studied curse and injury,
      we had what we called fun.

A boy's desire is to replace
      his tender heart with stone.
He wants his mother's worried hands
      wrung down to the bone.

He wants his father's sad old eyes
      to say *Don't be like me.*
He wants that man to warn him hard,
      and to ignore his plea.

We were brave in face of fear,
      we were brave and proud.
We played it cool, but we were false,
      for every boy's afraid.

We loved our moms; we loved our dads,
      but hated them, the same.
We envied them and pitied them,
      and became what they became.

PISSED ON

Children at the hands of children suffer wrong,
as I did when I was pissed on
by one of the neighbor boys I played among.
He leaped onto a log and flung
his piss-stream at me as I turned around.
He laughed at how he'd struck me dumb
by doing a thing I'd never imagined being done.

We are inadequate to what we do, to what is done
to us. I did nothing but walk slowly home
and stand in the shower for too long.
I've never wished him ill. (I found
him ill enough.) But, for his sake, not my own—
for his sake, I swear it, I have wished he'd never done
what he has done.

INTIMATIONS

and there was green
                    bamboo—
lithe spires shining
                    and smooth as river rocks
tumbled upwards into a flurry
of thin leaves,
                    interwoven branches
like legs of monstrous stick-bugs,
knotted at the joints,
                    and green and living
and grotesquely growing there and

trunks
        no boy could wrap his hands around,
and there were brown
                    young shoots,
tender obelisks, pyramidal,
                    that we would slice
from the moldering soil,
swinging staffs of cut bamboo
                    on which a hatchet
was of little use
                    except to fray
the sap-filled, impossibly tough stalks,
hollow and sinister—
                    they required a hacksaw,
but there were those that we would never touch
at the center of the forest of bamboo,
                    ancient trees, a congregation
of elders one hardly dared approach,
                    perhaps ten or fewer old ones
left lordly over what remained
                    of the forest they had sprung
and from the soft moldy floor of leaves
                    a stink

pervaded that grove,
                    white fungus working
in the moist dark at generations of leaves
and we were but children among ancient children

and I have been intimate always with death

ELUSIVE ANIMAL, CARRY ME

Sleepless night—
                 sudden vision:
a deer,
       elusive anim-
al, standing behind a tree,
a buck huge beyond
                   the scope
of actuality, antlers,
disproportionately immense, mingling
with the gray branches.
                  Then the image
stepped aside,
            replaced
by what had occupied my mind—
troubling questions in the shapes
of trees—
            If hell is
real, and I were damned,
                  could I prefer
annihilation, the end
              of existing, to
eternal pain?
          And a leafless
thought I hardly dared to climb—
If God is,
         could it be better
that He were not?
          I found
myself at the swaying top
of the tree, and was startled
at how desperately
            I clung
when the branches where I perched
began to carry me away,
              part

of a muscled beast, a mind,
whose antlers hold me
high, draw me through the woods,
so that I dare not lose my hold
but learn to love this grip.

A SHAPE WITH FORTY WINGS

Love is strange and calls me to stranger things.
When I was young I thought that I'd know why.
I've drawn my life—a shape with forty wings.

The woods at night are full of awesome beings.
Listen carefully and you can hear them cry:
Love is strange and calls us to stranger things.

I want to follow everything that sings,
but I cannot tell you how afraid I am to fly.
I've drawn my life—a shape with forty wings.

The unseen Being deep inside me brings
ideas to mind I hope I'll never try—
Love is strange and calls me to stranger things.

Possibilities surround me in concentric rings.
A light shines down that I cannot see by,
yet I've drawn my life—a shape with forty wings.

I walk about as if I understood my wanderings.
If You are near, show me how to die.
Love is strange and calls me to stranger things.
I've drawn my life—a shape with forty wings.

II.

Babel's Child

BABEL'S CHILD

*"Come, let us build for ourselves
a city and a tower . . ."*
—Genesis 11:4

We envied the sun—
                    its celestial status,
its effortless renown—
                    an apparatus
of glory, born
                    as fire is born, revealer
revealed in
                    its act of revelation. Sure,
we sensed it was a brute—
                    machine of God.
That was the root
                    of our designs, we who stood
rooted to the earth.
                    We dreamt of ways to climb.
Thus the birth
                    of our machinations. We had time
in those days,
                    when men lived several hundred years,
to rival the very rays
                    of the sun, which sneers
at an age of humankind.
                    Words we had to bind
our intentions, to wind
                    the rope of ambition around
our own necks.
                    A tower
we would make
                    to demonstrate the power
of the human will—
                    that was the extent of our force.
Even we could not still
                    God's sun in its course.

19

But out of words
                    we constructed dreams upon a bed
of deep desire. Hordes
                    of architects assembled,
speaking shared
                    words, meeting shared need.
We drafted
          lofty plans
                    that the sun and God would heed.

FLOCCINAUCINIHILIPILIFICATION

—The act of considering something worthless

One wonders how such words were coined.
A linguist was bored one day,
tired of translating Latin, Greek, Sanskrit,

his pencil straying to the borders of the page
as he wondered if his life would ever reach
beyond that desk, perhaps out the window.

Children scrambled out of a yellow bus
into the sun, onto the grass, between the trees—
such simple words, so compact, precise.

He needed something exorbitant
that he could repeat to himself, whisper
to unabridged dictionaries, scribbled pages, blunted pencils,

something he could shout at the bus driver
pulling away from the curb,
out the window if he ever chose to open it.

BORN AT SEA

            Culture's keel
thrusting forward
            in the wind of time:

            We steer a ship
we did not build,
            we shake down sails
as blank as our idea
            of how they came to be.

BIRTH

       In love
you were
         conceived,
in love
     brought forth
through the rent
          and bloodied
curtain
     of the flesh.
In violence
       you were
conceived,
       in violence
brought forth
        through the chamber
of the body
      into
a harsh world,
       being
vulnerable,
      being
of the flesh,
      prone
to love,
     vulnerable
to love's terrible violence.

ACHE

Recurring ache
in my belly, deep
in my back, reaching
through my groin—
I can't help but feel
that I'm growing old
so young—that soon
I'll long to stop living
just so I can finally
stop dying.

NEWSPAPER PHOTO

A picture of children skipping
in Africa through a swarm of locusts,

barely visible white
teeth, flailing arms and legs.

Only children know how
to play in a plague.

I SHOCKED THE HILLS

The eye is not satisfied with seeing,
nor the ear filled with hearing.
    —Ecclesiastes 1:8

A stream-bed mostly dry receded far
into the woods between two hills,
its water-fashioned rocks within the flow
of autumn leaves, a stream gone still.

I waded through the leaves, scared a deer
and a porcupine. I heard the hills'
caves moaning slightly in the wind. I felt
my body plant itself and bend, and still

I wanted more than that excess.
I gazed around, then shocked the hills,
breaking rock on rock in search of quartz—
in search of beauty, I would not be still.

BEAUTIFUL ANYWAY

There was a war
and most died.
The remaining ten
were taken as they gazed
at the sky, its radiant blue,
its magnitude.
The bomb that killed them
burst in flames
bright and glorious—
the last abomination.

As they had known it would,
the sun kept on
lighting up the sky and trees.
And it all kept on being
beautiful anyway.

PORTRAIT OF MYSELF AS A BARBARIAN

In some barbarous century
long before the invention
of eyeglasses, I stumble
from the fireside,
invisible hands extended,
heading for my hut,
but in the wrong direction.
Imagine my surprise when a tree
meets my hand
instead of a doorway hide,
when my humming becomes
the only human sound.
Imagine the way I laugh
at myself, tripping
through woods full
of phantom impediments—
the way I laugh, as the unseen
wolves advance upon me.

THE DEATH THE SUN WILL DIE

The terror of desire
is the opposite of the terror of fire,
which dies when deprived
and must be fed to grow.
In deprivation, desire flares,
growing to fill the void.

Like gold, I glow
in the forgery of desire.
How often I have rehearsed
the death the sun will die
in the emptiness of space.
Is there no other way to shine?

PLEASE FOLLOW THE INSTRUCTIONS

Read carefully
and pay attention
because we're gonna move,
my friend, for a moment
or two, so step
with me if you will.
We're on our way,
we're making progress,
smooth and steady now.
We're building a momentum
much smaller than a heavy train's,
gliding in the night,
but momentum nonetheless.
Now, slow
down, slow down,
and at my cue stop and read
from the bottom of the page up—
Ok, stop and begin again
at the last line *now*.

      reversal.
      this unforeseen
      through the page,
      this ascent
      of our downward trend,
      this abandonment
      of direction,
      this change
      for you and me—
      I had in store
      in mind, all
      This is all I had
      with new momentum.
      We're moving again
      Good, very good.
      this eccentric motion?
      Have you followed
      each other again?
      Have we found
      you're reaching for.
      Yes, this is the hand

HERALD

for Dad

Beneath the shroud of my fear
you'd enter into my night
when sleep was distant as the stars

and all comfort fell
like a meteor through the dark
and disappeared. You'd enter

singing and picking the guitar
you bought for almost nothing in Vietnam.
How did you learn songs to call the dawn,

train your voice to summon the nearest star?
Who taught you to play peace-invoking tunes
on a worn-out war-time guitar?

If I dared, I'd play now for you,
meet you in the dark
to recall to you our home

waiting beyond mourning
like Ithaca over the sea.
But I know no song to sing.

Your night I can't navigate,
where constellations can't cohere.
Your night I can't know.

I know only the distance of the stars,
the speed of a meteor to die.
In the onrush of your evening

this is the song I sing.
Nothing else I have to call out in the night,
to softly herald dawn.

THE SORROW OF MY FATHER

Even when he's joyful, he's sad.
In fact, he's sadder then,
as if his little joys remind him of his grief,
exceptions to a never-ending rule.
Such a paltry thing as joy could never make him glad.
When I last saw him he was standing alone at a window
thinking, I suppose, of how she had left.
Not knowing I was there, he smiled softly to himself—
and he was sad, he was sad, he was sad!

LAMENT

It began as a joke about aliens.
I claimed to have been contacted
by extra-terrestrial beings.
She played along, as expected,

what I took to be humor gracing her face
like light off water. I kept my cool,
detached air as long as possible.
She had not been taken into space,

but had been visited in the boughs
of a tree she'd climbed
and had seen another dimension of time
by looking into startled eyes.

She had a friend, a witness, who had watched
the creature hit the ground and run away.
She felt the thrill and fear again,
she told me, just knowing that I knew the way

she felt. A sudden sickness
shook me—this was no fiction—
not in her mind, anyway.
I had to betray her with my confession.

Her smile failed. "It's about trust,"
she said into her hands. *If I had known
you weren't joking* . . . was the best
I could think to say. "I could tell you I was kidding,"

she said wearily. *No*, I said, *don't lie.*
Then I left her, as I had to, with the awful truth
that she was alone, not known—a fact
too much of this world, too much of this Earth.

Lake Charles, March 17, 2006

FAILURE

makes itself at home
wherever you are. It is at ease.
It's as intimate
as a disease, as aloof
as a cat already fed.
It's underfoot. It's overhead.
It's in your way. It's at
your back. It's sudden
and unhurried. It taps
you on the shoulder.
It shakes your left hand.
It turns you around and it takes
your belt. It knows your name
but calls you something else.
It sits and watches
your reflection in the mirror.
It writes your signature
on every form you turn in,
on every painting you complete.

A BROKEN SONG

All my life I've tried to be
eloquent, saavy.
It seems to me it's time to lose
the ruse.

I've always looked down upon
simple songs, three chords long,
but all that's left for me to play
is F, A minor, and C.

I've sought glory for myself,
in the name of God I've loved myself.
I've never let two words rhyme
that are the same.

I'm getting older now,
old enough to say farewell
and piss on my broken attempts
at monuments.

All my life I've tried to be
worthy of glory,
but now I'm just trying to do
what will make me worthy of you.

EAGER PROPHET

God's prophets
              in the Old Testament were reluctant
to speak, pleading
                not me, not me.
Moses volunteered
               his brother,
who spoke more clearly.
                  Jonah wanted
to edit the message of the Most High.
                      Isaiah called
into question his own cleanliness,
                his merit,
before acceding in the end.

Not I—
        I watch the world,
my heart quickens as if to say,
                  pick me, pick me,
yet feeling already chosen.
              I sense a voice
rising through me
            and kick up my feet
like Balaam's dumb
           ass, braying on the road.

THE VOICE OF ONE CRYING OUT

I was wrong, when in desperation
I cried out,

> *I have so much to say to you—*
> *you who go on living*
> *as if living will go on—*
> *but not much you will take*
> *to heart, or even understand.*

Could I not see
that even morbid, fearful creatures
like me do their best to live
as if living will go on?
How could I have thought to condemn
because of *that*? And I was wrong
in my estimation of your eagerness
to take truth to heart, your capacity
for understanding, which, I now see,
is far greater than my own.
All those years I was carrying the message
from the hand of God
and shouting it out loud
on the streets,
I never once turned over
that tiny slip of paper
with God's name on it
and saw on the other side
not the name of the world
but my own name.

LAST REQUEST

Not the plastic blinds on the bedroom windows
nor the diamond on the antique ring,
but the translucent maple leaves in autumn,
yellow and luminous for an hour.
To have a body capable of being inhabited by light,
to diminish and yet receive—Oh, to die thus!

III.

Weak Devotions

Nevertheless, you must sing.
—the angel to Caedmon (cf. Bede's *Historia Ecclesiastica*)

WEAK DEVOTIONS

I.

Why do You leave
some recess of my mind,
my heart, unlorded?
Leave nothing behind
that will linger in shit
and wallow and grind
itself in filthy defiance,
in masochistic, blind
groping after further
blasphemies. Furnace, kind
Lord, the furthest reaches
of me—make me refined.
Make me new. Take me to You.
Why have You assigned
this torture to me,
this desperate mind
that thinks inevitably
what it fears to think? Be kind
and do not let me be.
Need I remind
You, Lord, that You lay claim
to even the blindness of the purblind
worm—not only its righteous
wriggling? Be kind and be, kind
Lord, what You rightly are.
Rule what—whatsoever—you find.
Rein me in and reign in me.
There is freedom only when You bind.
Take me wholly, holy God.
Wholly, Holy. Mind my mind.

II.

Religion is a Crutch

but not at first—first it is the diagnosis
and the medication prescribed,
it is the scalpel and the surgeon's hand,
it is the surgery and the hospital bed,
the death of anesthesia and the waking up.
And yes it is the crutch by which one heals
and learns to walk and live all over again.
And you say *crutch* as if it were an easy thing.

III.

In my mind there is a population of squirrels
in a field of doubt, each one a question
about You. They are not pretty squirrels.
They are mangy, trembling things with teeth.
They are rummaging in the grass and darting
up and down the trees, gnawing and twitching.
But when they feel the wind of Your passing,
they freeze where they are and lean back on their haunches,
hands folded in front, asking forgiveness.
They become so beautiful I forget they're mine.

IV.

Sometimes I'm afraid that I am damned
by God. Such blasphemies have entered my mind
as I dare not repeat for fear of making others stumble.
And once something enters my mind,
I have to wonder if it originated in my heart.
(Let it not be so!)
                              Sometimes the only relief
is this feeling that, even if I were damned,
I would say: If it be Your will, may it be so.
Is this something someone who was damned
would say—or hope to say?

V.

Our holiest act is to enter into mystery,
just as God's holiest act was to enter
into mortal flesh, into death—
the only mystery available to Him.

VI.

The Harrowing

not of Hell only, but of the earth,
and not in strength of arms, but in assumed
vulnerability, in mortal flesh,
in sacrifice. What kind of God creates
a world that will necessitate His own
suffering, His harrowing of Himself?
That God and no other would I have
harrow my heart and be hallowed in it.

VII.

Sometimes I don't want to praise You, Lord.
I'd rather let the stones cry out
and see if they can shame me into song,
rid me of my muting doubt.

Here's my voice in praise—though it seems wrong
for You to prefer my stony song to the stones' accord.

VIII.

Spring again.
>Rain showers beat the dogwood and lilac.
>Glory petals strew the path
>>of my undeserving.

He does not treat us as our sins deserve
or repay us according to our iniquities.

~

The next day, I walk by again.
>The petals are sliming in the sun,
stricken with flies,
>and the world is briefly
>telling the truth about me.

IX.

and if in spring it suddenly turns

       cold and a dead brown leaf scritches

    against a branch
               what
harsh thing
      are You saying to me

    over and again

X.

My heart is creaturely before You.

And if I am full of anger, have mercy.
And if I am crooked, remember me.
And if my thoughts are (all my thinking isisis)
perverse, release me from them.
And if I know love only from a fearful distance,
take me to You, writhing and undone.

I do not want I want I want I want
(kicking and yelping) Your law,
a leash around my neck. (Have mercy.)
Without it I am not fit for company.
Do not leave me
feral and alone—yank
my heart that it may come heeling
and creaturely before You.

XI.

Remember my partitioned
hearts, sevenly seeking to
love You, little seats for Your
smallest mercies to topple
in their lightest sitting down.

XII.

Anxiety Disorder; Major Depressive Disorder

I grew older. The terrors of my childhood—
anxious days, sleepless nights weeping,
gasping for breath, afraid of the strangeness
of death and afraid of the strangeness
of existence—became mostly a memory.
I thought I had become a man.
I thought I had learned how to live.
But You said, Look, you are a child again,
and in that moment I suffered Your terrors anew,
and they did not end. Month one. Month two. Month three.
Over and over I despaired of peace, of life itself.
You said, Look, you are a child again.
And in my self-pity and in my anger
I was not listening. You terrified me,
You terrified me, You brought me down
into the pit. And You said, Look,
you are a child again. And I said,
How dare You? I cannot endure.
And You said, Nevertheless.
And I said, Why? And I raged
and I shook and I wept for weeks,
and then I fell silent in my despair.
And You said, Look, you are a child again,
and now you can call me Father.

XIII.

I have envied, yes,
the dog that cannot think of hell—
I have envied the dust mite,
the palm tree and the stone.
And can I say
(can I tell You something
I've never told You before?)
that I have envied nonthings
because they do not exist.

XIV.

There is so much anger in me
because we are mortal and suffer
in body and soul—
I am full of bile,

but won't You turn it into sweetness?
If You can make honey
in the carcass of a lion,
can't You do this in me?

XV.

Though there is a sorrow comes
that cannot be dissuaded
and a fear that will not subside,
beauty insists—
            little imperfect trumpet
of God's glory blown into purple bloom
on the chain-link fence. And you see it.

IV.

The Voice of One Crying Out

CHOIRMASTER

I require of you the fat man, the farter, the spastic drooling on her sleeve.
Come, chain-smokers. Bring the deaf boy and his grandfather.
Where is the man with the artificial voice box? I need him now.
Have so few rappers come? Call them. Get them here.
Assemble the children and their cats and dogs.
I want the lisper in this section on my right.
Call the nurses at the nursing homes to wheel the bedridden in.
I need the coughers and the burpers right here beside the shrill old ladies.
Run to the door one last time. Call people from the street.
Any who come are fit to stay. The hour is upon us.
The drunks in the back row have already begun their ruckus.
The yodlers and the karaoke enthusiasts can hardly contain themselves.
This is the Gloria Patri. If you can sing, sing.
If you can only croak, croak like you've never croaked before.

SOJOURNER'S PRAYER

A little landing, Lord, a covered ledge
in your castle, a stoop in your pagoda,
an inconspicuous nook in your great house—

an alcove in your palace of unnumbered rooms,
a place at the sideboard in your hall of infinite length—

the tiniest tent in the unending field of your glory,
a lean-to in the woods of your praise—

one half of a bench on the footpath of your garden,
a single stump at the edge of your lawn—

a miniscule plot of land, a rock
beneath the star-shingled sky of your roof—

one foot on the ground you possess, one finger
grasping a blade of grass within the border of your kingdom,
my simple heart at the very outskirts of your reign.

PATIENT'S PRAYER

The test was positive, by which
I mean, oh God, you know, the news
was negative. But what you mean
by all of this I can't conceive.
Remember when I wasn't yet?
And then you did a thing I can't forget,
or quite forgive—not yet.
You remember, don't you,
when I was born? Do you
regret, well, me?
                        The doctors
said the name of this disease,
and I said it back, but incorrectly,
imperfectly, on purpose—
like an Artist, making a beautiful mistake.

CONDUCTOR'S PRAYER

May I never lose my place
in a sprawling symphony,
or fling my baton in a cellist's face
when I get carried away. May funny
gestures look like genius. Please,
let eyes be lifted up to me
from time to time, to ease
my sense of being unnecessary.

Don't let me fall off my dais.
May multiple movements
hold together as a piece. Let long
performances end in silence
then applause. But more
than all of these, just let there
be music when I move,
even if the movement's wrong.

DANCERS' PRAYER

God of the drive to pirouette,
of the thousandth bow,
the unending bending of the knees,
the muscles seizing up without cease,
the release of stepping into stinging water,
hot and barely bearable—
                                        God
of practice and of punishment,
of extra hours spent in spending
ourselves, God of power
in muscles used after they refused
at first,
            God of the worst
tours en l'air, the mediocre *entrechats*
and all the rest, all the necessary
mess we make to make ourselves
progress, until the moment, God,
when we cease to merely hope
                                        to be,
when we become, oh God-Of-That-Success,
and cease to be mere witnesses,
when the lights ignite, adrenaline
sets the heart alight, muscles
awake, and we abandon
                                ideas
and every conception of beauty
in order to participate,
to no longer see, but to be
part
        of it.

HEDONIST'S PRAYER

I was in love with my own ruin, in love with decay . . . .
—Augustine, *Confessions* (Book II, 4.9)

Our Father in heaven, hallowed be the natural
man here below. Lead me in the path of pleasure.
May my will be done and make of earth a heaven.
Upon my instincts I meditate day and night,
I study to fulfill their decrees. Nature's law
is my delight, the satiation of desire.
But thus far I've failed, as if desire's gut
were growing larger than my own. I've fed it
smut and sex, paid dearly for the finest luxuries,
but yearning is thus burned away, leaving me singed
and dry as cinders, Lord.
                    What wine or whiskey
will purge my gaping throat? I sought counsel
in the house of sinners, was welcomed heartily,
and I spoke, wind escaping the pit prepared for me
within my own chest. Deliver me from craving,
this lust for emptiness—fill me up, dear God,
even though (*dear God!*) I'm overflowing.
This table, this plate, this bottomless fucking bottle—
I'm fed up, oh Lord. I have become
a law unto myself—forbid, Father,
in your mercy, that I should keep it.

AMATEUR'S PRAYER

I picked up the guitar
for a week and a day.
I didn't get very far.
But I learned to play
a few songs softly,
in my own halting way.
I didn't want anything grand
—a simple tune I could carry,
something ready to hand,
beautiful, but not very.

THE OLD PREACHER PRAYS

There are few words
left sufficient to this world.
Darkness among the meadowed hills
and light along the rock-strewn ridge
are expressive in my mind as words
can no longer be. When I want to pray,
I peer after a thunderstorm
through hung fog into the sun—
I go looking for the means afforded:
oaks and asphalt and sunken creekbeds . . .
I watch the world, and You hear.

TENDENCY

Here's the precious chill,
the liquid current.
Delight slinks downstream.
Soft metal, quick
silver. Veil of steel.
I kneel and sink
under. Everywhere
umbra. Muted resonance.
My body becomes
a larger body,
flows.
          There is death
down here, and terror,
its cohort. I don't want to be
danced down the rocky riverbed.
A hard, hard thing it is
to make myself stay under.
Long. Longer. Growing
cold. Hold
the fear, bear
it, unbearable.
A hard, hard thing.
But harder to convince
myself that I can come up
again, that I can be
forgiven,
          though the current
is already turning my face
into unearned air.

WISTERIA

When wisteria has taken the tree,
strangled the boughs in its arms,
its petals brimming in the breeze,
you grip me, sweet
sensibility. Take me
in your unrelenting hands,
grow through this scaffolding of bones
up to the sweetening sun—
I give myself over.
Climb, here, and secure your hold.
Take me down, wrapped
in the power of your aroma,
your coloring of the light
as you flower high in the sun.
Let the tree become nothing
but what rises through it.

Notes

"Hedonist's Prayer": The epigraph from Augustine is from Maria Boulding's translation.

"Eager Prophet": See Numbers 22: "When the donkey saw the angel of Yahweh, she lay down under Balaam; so Balaam was angry and struck the donkey with his stick. And Yahweh opened the mouth of the donkey. . . ."

About the Author

Luke Hankins (b. 1984) grew up in Louisiana before moving to North Carolina as a teenager, where he now permanently resides. He attended the Indiana University MFA in Creative Writing program, where he held the Yusef Komunyakaa Fellowship in Poetry. He is Senior Editor at *Asheville Poetry Review*, where he has served on staff since 2006. He is the editor of an anthology of poems entitled *Poems of Devotion: An Anthology of Recent Poets*, forthcoming from Wipf & Stock in 2012. A chapbook of his translations of French poems by Stella Vinitchi Radulescu, *I Was Afraid of Vowels . . . Their Paleness*, was published by Q Avenue Press in 2011. His poems, essays, and translations have appeared in numerous publications, including *American Literary Review, Contemporary Poetry Review, New England Review, Poetry East, St. Katherine Review*, and *The Writer's Chronicle*, as well as on the blog of the National Public Radio program *Being*.

misrepresented people:
public responses to
Trump's America
(2018)